Two Nativity Dramas

EDWARD S. LONG

"THE TINSEL TIME MACHINE"
"RAG DOLL NUMBER THIRTY SEVEN"

C.S.S. Publishing Company
Lima, Ohio

TWO NATIVITY DRAMAS

S852.5t
4874/ISBN 0-89536-697-5   PRINTED IN U.S.A.

The Tinsel Time Machine

Production Notes

A minimum of characters are needed.

No elaborate costuming, make-up, or stage setting are involved.

The play can be performed in chancel or on stage.

"Extras" may be readily incorporated at the last minute (wearing winter coats) into the "carolers" in the England segment.

It can be performed books in hand, or some or all of the cast may wish to memorize their lines.

Only three rehearsals are needed for an effective presentation.

The action is simple. The actors and actresses are urged to put feeling and expression into each line and movement, rather than rushing through to "get it over with".

The humor in the play makes it appropriate for both teenage young people and adult participants.

Effects

The Tinsel Time Machine can be constructed from a cardboard box. It should have a light inside (a flashlight), dials, and tinsel here and there. It needs to look interesting (the youth could build one).

For light and sound when the time machine operates, simply flick lights off and on rapidly (a strobe light could be used). For sound, record a vacuum cleaner and amplify it over the PA system.

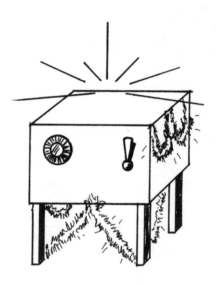

Cast of Characters

TOM: Twelve-year-old son of Mr. and Mrs. Randall. He is unhappy about Christmas because his father is laid off and presents will be few.

TINA: Tom's fourteen-year-old sister. She shares some of Tom's mood, but appears a little more philosophical about it.

LENNY: Her real name is Lenora. A "whiz kid," she's a close friend of Tina and about the same age.

MR. RANDALL: Works in a large factory near Shadybrook, but at this Christmas season finds himself laid off.

MRS. RANDALL: Doing her best to provide income by taking on a part-time job packing and sorting eggs. She tries to keep up the family spirit, but by Christmas Eve her spirit is badly depleted.

KLAUS KINDERMANN: A German tailor imprisoned by the Nazis in a camp somewhere in Germany, in 1944. A friend of Dietrich Bonhoeffer.

CAROLERS: Various ages of young people going from house to house singing and hoping for treats or money in England in the year 1820.

JIMMY YEOMAN: Young English lad with whom the children strike up a conversation.

INNKEEPER: The man who operates the Inn where Mary and Joseph sought lodging the first Christmas night.

INNKEEPER'S WIFE: She seems to be having regrets about having had to turn Mary and Joseph away, is glad to have helped them, and is anxious to talk to the travelers about that night and the events of the following days.

NARRATOR: It is Christmas Eve in the small town of Shadybrook, a picturesque town nestled in rolling farm fields, yet in the distance one can see the smoke stacks of large industry. There is no snow, so that the lights and decorations lack some of the usual Christmas sparkle. At the Randall home, Tina and Tom are in a bleak mood. The family is gathered around the fireplace as Mrs. Randall knits absent-mindedly. The plant where Mr. Randall works has laid off most of its workers until February.

TOM: What a "turkey" this Christmas is going to be!!

MRS. RANDALL: Tom, that's not a nice way to talk. Even though it's been a rough year for us, it still is Christmas. We have each other. We're well. And, anyway, the real meaning of Christmas doesn't depend on lots of presents.

TINA: I hope not Mom. Look at that pitiful collection under the tree; I think those drooping branches are trying to cover the hard, bare facts.

MR. RANDALL: Tom! Tina! *(He drops his newspaper to his lap and gives them a glare which indicates disapproval).*

TINA AND TOM: *(After looking down in shame).* We're sorry!

MR. RANDALL: I know what you're feeling. When I was a boy there was one Christmas, when our farm was quarantined because Sis had smallpox. All I got that year was a pair of socks and some lead pencils for school. You see, they wouldn't let us sell our milk or eggs. In fact, until after Christmas we couldn't leave the farm. *(He muses).* I can still see Mom putting some money under a rock by the mailbox with a note that Mr. Smith would take to town. He'd bring us things we needed — and just leave them at the end of the lane.

TINA: Oh, Dad, I know that. You've told us that story before. But I'm still disappointed.

TOM: I know there've been rough times at Christmas through the years. But I wish I could be sure people really did find the Christmas meaning in spite of everything.

TINA: Maybe someday Lenny will invent a time machine and she can take us back to see . . .

MRS. RANDALL: Listen, everybody: it's eleven o'clock, and if we're going to the Christmas sunrise service, we'd all best get on to bed.

TOM: Mom, I don't know if I want to go . . . to church, I mean. *(Looks nervously at her).*

MRS. RANDALL: *(Sighs)* Well, we'll wake you just in case you change your mind. You're old enough, I guess we shouldn't force you any more.

TOM: G'night Mom, Dad.

TINA: 'Night, everybody. *(They exit).*

MR. RANDALL: Remember when they used to hug and kiss us when they went to bed? I guess they're growing up.

(MR. and MRS. RANDALL exit. TOM and TINA come back on stage with blankets, as if going to bed. The stage is dark).

LENNY: *(After a period of silence; in stage whisper).* Tina! Tina!

TINA: *(Comes to porch window).* Lenny, what are you doing on our porch roof? *(Rubs sleep from her eyes).*

LENNY: Slip some clothes on, I've got something to show you in our garage.

TOM: *(Sticks his head out of his window).* Hey, Lenny what the dickens . . . ?

LENNY: Get dressed Tom and come with us. *(After a pause all exit).*

NARRATOR: The scene is now Lenny's garage, which she calls her "laboratory." Tools, piles of wood, strands of wire, birdhouses, bicycles and a lawnmower surround her work space.

LENNY: There . . . (She gestures to the Tinsel Time Machine). It works.

TOM: It "works"? What does it do?

LENNY: Takes a person back in time.

TINA: How 'bout forward?

LENNY: Nope, only back and then a return to now. So far at least.

TOM: You're kidding. Did you drag me from my warm bed for some kinda' joke? The greatest scientists can't do that! How can you? Birdhouses and crystal sets, maybe, but . . .

LENNY: We were putting up our Christmas tree. I was dancing around in my slippers, creating static electricity. As I danced and whirled, I wound tinsel around me. Suddenly I was back in time — to my first Christmas, when we hung our stockings from the fireplace the first time. Mom and Dad looked younger and everything. (She pauses as she points at the machine). Tinsel, wires and electricity. Where'd you like to go?

TOM: How do we do it?

LENNY: First everyone has to get on a chair, and the chair has to be hooked up with a string of tinsel. Then there are two dials to set before pulling this lever: One dial is for the year and one for the country. Let's see what it was like thirty-five years ago when our parents were little — 1944 (Sets dial) . . . in Germany (Sets dial).

TOM: How about where, Lenny? Germany's a big place, after all!

LENNY: Sorry 'bout that . . . Hang on! Here we go! (She pulls the

lever. The lights go out, lights within the time machine come on —
house lights go off and on several times. After a pause they slowly
come on).

NARRATOR: As the Time Machine comes to rest we find our-
selves in a dark, low-ceiling building. Illumination comes only
from a few electric bulbs hanging from the ceiling. There are
metal doors and many iron-fence dividers. Behind one such
barrier we find one man . . .

KLAUS: *(Singing to himself or to whomever is listening).* Stille
nacht, heilige nacht . . . *(Stops as he sees the children).* Weigehtz!
["Vee-gates"]

TOM: Weigehtz! "The gate's okay, but the hinge is rusty", as my
uncle says.

KLAUS: Aha! you sound American. But how did you get in here?

LENNY: That's hard to explain. But is it Christmas Eve? And
who are you?

KLAUS: My name is Klaus. I am a German, a tailor by trade. I
am imprisoned — for a year now — for opposing the Nazis and
the Fuehrer.

TOM: You . . . you mean Hitler?

KLAUS: Ach, so you know of him too. At first we in the church
thought him no harm. Then as time went on and he engaged us
in a world war and put Jews and dissenters in camps, we began to
oppose him. Ja, that landed me here, awaiting trial. And it is
hard to be here at Christmas time. We are not allowed to
worship formally, although when the guards are friendly we sing,
pray or talk from cell to cell. Pastor Bonhoeffer writes a lot and
says we must exist in faith without the trappings of religion . . .
but I'd like to be able to have a real church service — with Com-
munion. One of the guards promised us a nice Christmas roast
tomorrow . . .

TOM: (Thoughtfully). Bonhoeffer . . . our Pastor, often refers to him in sermons . . .

KLAUS: Then, then you are from the future? Could that be . . . ? I hear a guard coming. You must leave. Schnell, go quickly!

LENNY: Come on, everybody! Step on it! Back to the machine!

KLAUS: But tell me first, is Hitler finally defeated? Does the war end?

TINA: Yes to both Mr. Klaus. Goodbye!

KLAUS: Gott sei Dank. Aufwiedersehen *[Owf-VEE-der-zay-un]* Goodbye to you.

TOM AND LENNY: Goodbye. And Merry Christmas!

(The lights go off and the machine lights up again).

TINA: (In the darkness). Where are we now?

LENNY: I set the machine for England, 1820.

NARRATOR: The scene is one as if from a Christmas card: little houses with glowing windows; streets and trees and yards bedecked with snow. Now and then a horse-drawn sleigh whooshes by, with padded hoofbeats and jingling harness or bells. A few little shops appear closed for the night. Some children are caroling, you can hear them now.

CAROLERS: (Singing).

> What child is this, Who laid to rest,
> On Mary's lap is sleeping?
> Whom angels greet with anthems sweet,
> While shepherds watch are keeping?
>
> This, this is Christ the King,
> Whom shepherds guard and angels sing:

Haste, haste to bring Him laud,
The Babe, the Son of Mary!

JIMMY: (To the **CAROLERS***)*. Must be goin' now. Mama said to
be straight-a-way home at midnight to light the candles, and for
plum pudding. *(Stops short when he sees the children)*. Oh Lordy,
you gave me a fright . . . who are you?

TINA: We're from America — and twentieth century.

JIMMY: (Looks dubiously at them). Well, even with the dim light I
can see you're different lookin'. I'm Jimmy Yeoman. I'm sixteen
and lookin' to be in Her Majesty's Navy. I do enjoy singin' on
Christmas Eve; and I enjoy our plum pudding. You see we're a
poor lot — the Yeomans — Daddy died from too much coal dust
and Mama takes in washing. I work in the mines, but the Navy
has promised to take me next year. I got Mama and little Sis
each a raisin cake — from the bakery.

TOM: You are unfortunate! Just think! No Star Wars outfits. No
racing sets. No football gear!

JIMMY: A different sort of life you've got, I wager. But we've got
the candle service at the Abbey and we're just glad to be alive, a'
livin' on coal choppin' and clothes-scrubbin'. I, I'd best be
goin' . . .

TINA: I wish we could stay too. You're cute! Merry Christmas!
TOM and *LENNY join in with her)*. Merry Christmas!

JIMMY: (Turns). Oh, by the by. Do . . . do we Britishers and you
in America stay friends?

TOM: (Shouts). Yes, we do! *(JIMMY smiles, waves and exits)*.

LENNY: It's getting late. But we have time for one more visit.

TINA: Let's go to Bethlehem, back then when the Baby was
born. You don't suppose our looking in on it would be sac . . . sac
. . . sacrificious . . . ?

LENNY: Sacrilegious? Well, I don't think so. But there's a problem — two problems actually. *(TINA* and *TOM* groan). For one thing, it would only be by luck that we'd set down in Bethlehem. For another, there's the date: figuring the calendar changes, the birth of Jesus is sometimes calculated as early as 6 BC or as late as AD 4. Remember? The Pastor said that in Confirmation class.

TOM: How about splitting the difference and going back to AD 1?

LENNY: Okay, hang on. Here we go . . . Let's just hope we're lucky!

(Again the lights go out; they flicker on again as the machine's lights go off).

NARRATOR: The scene is a rocky hillside near Bethlehem in Judea. We have come to rest in front of a sort of cave in a hillside, a cavern which is obviously fashioned into a stable. The sky is bright and there are thousands of stars overhead. A few large buildings are silhouetted against the sky on the hill above, a dim light visible in the open windows here and there. The night is warm and the wind balmy.

TINA: Wow, it's warm, just like in Florida. We sure wouldn't freeze here when we went Christmas caroling!

TOM: (Mysteriously) Hey! Do you think that . . . that cave over there could be the stable?

LENNY: It's possible. But we're either too late or too early. *(They walk closer).*

TOM: It feels special, like the inside of a church. But it's empty. There's only a little straw — no sign of animals having been here lately.

TINA: (Looks at the manger). Do . . . do you think this could be the same manger where Jesus was born? *(They are reverently silent, looking at the manger).*

INNKEEPER: (With a lantern). I thought I heard voices. What are you doing here?

LENNY: (Jumps). You sure scared me, Mister! We mean no harm. We hoped to find the stable where the Baby was born.

INNKEEPER'S WIFE: About two years ago there was an enrollment, when Quirinias was governor of Syria. Lots of people were on the road then. A man and a woman came to find room in our inn. We had no room. When they were turned away, I felt so badly I suggested the stable. They took me up on the offer. The baby was born, but not in this manger. It was in the old one, which finally fell apart. I — we — came down each day some to see if they were okay. There was a star or bright light. There were shepherds. There were strange wealthy men from the East on camels. All of them came and worshiped the Baby and congratulated the parents as if they knew them.

TINA: How come you don't take better care of this special place?

TOM: (Scolding). Tina!

INNKEEPER: That's all right. We would like to. But, you see, we heard of Herod's order to kill all new boys just after the baby was born. Someone heard he asked the wealthy visitors to report back to him when they had found the King. So we thought it would be wisest to not help Herod out. We heard the Baby and his parents escaped to Egypt. Who would want to harm babies?

LENNY: It sounds like you really became fond of Jesus and his family.

INNKEEPER'S WIFE: Jesus. Yes, that's what they named Him. Whatever happened to him, I wonder . . .

TOM: After a life of ministry and a death on a cross he rose and is alive in spirit yet. Millions of people recognize him as God's Son.

INNKEEPER: (Skeptically). How on earth would you know anything like that? Who *are* you anyway?

TINA: We're . . . well, we're from another century . . . one far in the future, actually. In our church we know him as God's Son and our Lord.

INNKEEPER: (Looking pleased). Oh, I'm glad to know that. And to know he escaped Herod.

LENNY: We'd better be going. (They turn toward the machine).

INNKEEPER'S WIFE: Oh, but tell me first, before you go: how are we — my husband and I — remembered? Do people hate us because we had no room in the inn?

TINA: Maybe a few people. But I think most people realize this humble birthplace identifies Jesus with the most common things or people. Your little stable is copied and painted and written about a great deal . . . But we must go. Goodbye! *(LENNY and TOM wave and say goodbye).*

INNKEEPER & WIFE: (They smile, relieved). Shalom, good friends! (They exit).

(The lights go out, flicker, go out again, and the machine shuts off; the Time Machine and chairs are taken away; TOM and TINA are back in bed).

MRS. RANDALL: (At the door to each of their bedrooms). Tom, Tina. It's 5 o'clock; we have to leave soon for church. Do you want to go?

MR. RANDALL: (Appears next to his wife, as TOM and TINA wake up). We'll take a nice drive through the country. And when we come home I'll make your favorite waffle breakfast . . . we'll have the best Christmas we can.

TINA: (Hesitantly). I . . . I had a dream . . . well anyway, I feel differently this morning. This can be a good Christmas I think. The meaning is still here.

TOM: Dad, Mom, I . . . I'm sorry I was so greedy-sounding. I know you love us and that you'll do anything for us. I feel like Tina. I'm positive this Christmas is special — especially for us . . .

NARRATOR: And for you too! The people in Shadybrook are waking up now. There, look: another string of lights is lit. Some, like the Randall family, are going to early church. The first light of dawn is coming into the eastern sky. Out in the country there are lights in some of the barns as farm folk begin their chores. Someone left a light on in the garage at Lenny's house. Oh, and although the sky is pink in the East, long gray clouds overhead are beginning to shower giant flakes of snow over the scene.

Merry Christmas!

Rag Doll #37

Production Notes

Simple props are used.
A flashlight may suffice for illuminating the scenes as the Rag
Dolls appear.
The Rag Dolls' costumes may be made by tacking small squares
of cloth over blue jeans, etc. Blush or rouge may be used on
cheeks to give the appearance of a simple, rag doll.

Cast of Characters

NARRATOR

MR. McKENZIE: A shopkeeper in his late 60s. Beginning to be a little stoop-shouldered. Wears glasses.

MRS. McKENZIE: Helps in the shop and makes the dolls.

GERALD: Young man about sixteen. He has worked for Mr. McKenzie for several years, and, now that he has his license, delivers groceries.

MAID: One of several servants at the Hibbing estate *(Her name is MRS. SMITH)*.

LAURA HIBBING: Only child of the Hibbings. Nearly seventeen. Alone in the large house on Christmas Eve, except for the servants.

RAG DOLLS, 17, 23, 1: Three dolls from the past.

CAROLERS: A group of children whose singing awakens Laura on Christmas morning *(They should wear coats, as if outdoors on a chilly morning)*.

NARRATOR: There's a cozy atmosphere around the wood-burning stove in the Quality Grocery in Midville. While snow flurries around the windows, Mr. and Mrs. McKenzie — who operate the store — and Gerald sit around the stove and drink hot chocolate. The business district is a small one, in the old section of this middle-sized town. The street is made of brick and the tires of passing vehicles make a distinctive buzzing sound.

MR. McKENZIE: What do you think, Ma? Should we turn this place into a supermarket? You know, I love this place and it brings all the income we'll ever need. But we're not very . . . you know . . . up to snuff. We're kind of out-of-date, you know what I mean?

MRS. McKENZIE: Whatever you want as long as I don't have to clean all them picture windows. Gracious, they'd be the death of me! *(Sews on a doll).*

GERALD: Oh, I'd clean 'em — or get Moose to do it. For a small fee. That guy is so tall, he'd never even need a ladder. *(Turns to MR. Mc and looks a little embarrassed).* But Boss, I hope you understand this the way I mean it: you're kind of out of date just like the store, and I don't think you'd be happy with a dozen check-outs, pre-packaged this and that . . . *(MR. Mc doesn't know how to take this).* Your store's name is real . . . "Quality" . . . that's what people get here. And the personal service and fresh-cut meats are old-fashioned in a good way, I reckon. Only place in the county that delivers groceries. And I'm proud to say it's me that delivers 'em.

MR. McKENZIE: Yes, I guess you're right. By the way, Gerald, I do have a delivery ready — for Mrs. Stone, over by the bridge. *(GERALD gets up and puts on his jacket).* Oh, and Gerald: take it easy on Old Bessie. That old van wasn't made to do wheelies!

GERALD: Don't worry, Boss. I'll be back in a flash with the cash. *(Exits).*

MRS. McKENZIE: There! The doll is ready to be given away. *(Holds it up and examines it proudly).* Every year you have that insight about what girl or boy needs a doll; but so far, this year, Pa, you haven't said "boo" about it . . .

MR McKENZIE: Nope. Ma, I just don't know. My mind tells me one thing, and my intuition hasn't changed since before Thanksgiving; but . . . it just doesn't sound . . . or seem . . . or feel right. *(Warms hands by the stove and thinks).* Well . . .

MRS. McKENZIE: Well, you gonna let me in on it or not?

MR. McKENZIE: The person who's been on my mind is Laura Hibbing . . . and that doesn't 'compute' as they say. Every year we've given a doll it's been different: usually a poor family, or a youngster in the hospital, or an orphan gits it. I just don't know . . .

MRS. McKENZIE: Gracious sakes, Pa. I know why your mind's befuddled: she's rich, and maybe a little old for dolls. She's seventeen or so, isn't she? Since they built the new mansion up at the Point, by the bay, I don't think I've seen her. Not since the time she came in with the maid for some special cuts for a big wing-ding they were a' havin' up there.

(GERALD comes back in).

MR. McKENZIE: Laura Hibbing, that's it though. *(He nods his head, as though agreeing with himself).*

GERALD: A delivery for the Hibbings? Right away! That Laura is so cute it would be worth the trip. Without pay, even. *(Moans).* But she'd never go out with me — in that heap I drive. Not with her havin' that stable full of thoroughbreds and those three sports cars. *(Moans again).* Oh, wow, Mr. McKenzie, is that who gets the doll this year? Golly, she might throw it back at us . . . I'm sorry, Mrs. McKenzie, but you know what I mean . . .

(MRS. Mc smiles and nods).

MR. McKENZIE: Well, if'n I don't change my mind, we'll take it to her after we close tomorrow — Christmas Eve.

GERALD: (*Imitates John Wayne*). Ya can count on me. Howdy, Miz Hibbing, Ma'am. Ya don't know me yet, but ya will.

(*Lights down*).

NARRATOR: All day December 24, as customers file through the Quality Grocery for last-minute items, Mr. McKenzie ponders. Evening finds Gerald and Mr. McKenzie driving up the long road from the gatehouse to the Hibbing residence. As they approach the door, large snowflakes whirl around the well-decorated entrance. They ring the doorbell.

(*Lights up*).

MAID: Deliveries out back . . . please. (*Does a double-take*). Oh, it's you Mr. McKenzie.

MR. McKENZIE: Beg your pardon for intruding on Christmas Eve, but I've a present for Laura.

MAID: (*Looks puzzled*). Why, certainly. Come in out of the snow. Mr. and Mrs. Hibbing are gone, on a cruise someplace. But they said to thank you for those good chops they had at the last party. Excuse me a second. (*MAID leaves to get LAURA. MR. McKENZIE and GERALD stand uncomfortably and GERALD spruces up his jacket and smooths his hair*).

GERALD: Maybe we could run for it before she gets back.

(*MAID and LAURA return*).

MAID: Now, Laura, this is Mr. McKenzie from the market. He says he has a gift for you. And this is . . .

MR. McKENZIE: Gerald, my helper at the store, ma'am. (*GERALD shifts uncomfortably*). Here, (*Hands LAURA the package*). for you from the Missus and me.

LAURA: Why I . . . I don't know what to say (*Momentarily off guard*). Mrs. Smith (*Hands it to the maid*), please take it to my

room. I'll open it sometime after dinner. Thank you . . . I guess
(She says to **MR. Mc** in cool tones). Good night. (Returns to another room).

MR. McKENZIE: (Feeling awkward). Well, Mrs. Smith, time to
go. Got a church service to get ready for . . . (Turns to leave);
GERALD stands, peering in the direction **LAURA** went).

MAID: Good night. And Merry Christmas. (Shrugs as if to apologize for **LAURA**).

MR. McKENZIE: Gerald! (**GERALD** snaps out of his reverie and
follows **MR. Mc** out).

(Lights Down).

NARRATOR: It is now nearly midnight and it is dark in Laura's
room, as she prepares to retire. The maid is turning down the
bedcovers.

(Lights partway up).

LAURA: Good night, Mrs. Smith. (She turns toward the bed, then
remembers the package; she opens it curiously). **A rag doll?** (In-
credulous, she laughs, then throws down the doll). **What on earth!**
(Seems to have second thoughts; picks up the fallen doll and tenderly holds it for a while). **Mr. McKenzie's a strange old duck** (Puts
doll on a chair) . . . **old store . . . crummy old truck. Hmm . . .**
(Snickers softly). **Gerald was kind of cute . . . poor, but cute . . .**
(She gets into bed, pulls covers up; all lights out).

RAG DOLL #17: Laura, Laura . . . (Light only on the doll; it calls
again in subdued tones). **Laura, Laura . . .**

LAURA: (Rises up, squinting). Hmmm? Who's there?

RAG DOLL # 17: It's me. I'm Rag Doll 17. From a Christmas
years ago . . .

LAURA: (Sleepily). That's nice. Now just go away so I can sleep,
please.

RAG DOLL # 17: First I must tell you my story. Then I will go.

LAURA: All right tell me the story *(Aside).* What am I saying? *(To the doll again).* But then get lost, take a hike . . .

RAG DOLL # 17: I only have a few minutes of life . . . Mr. and Mrs. McKenzie gave me to a little girl whose parents were divorced right before Christmas and she only got shoes and some gloves for Christmas. No tree. No daddy to tuck her in bed, and her mother cried most of the time. When she saw me she hugged me and squealed with delight. That Christmas Eve, and many many other nights, she hugged me all night as she slept. I was happy then — as happy as rag dolls can be. Now I'm on her bed in the college room and we're just like old friends . . . She's come such a long way since that dreadful Christmas . . . Oh my *(Light flickers).* Oh, oh I'm losing my power . . . *(Weakly).* Goodbye. Merry Christmas. *(Voice weaker).* Merry Christmas *(Lights out; voice weaker yet).* Merry Christmas . . .

LAURA: Good riddance and good night! *(Snuggles into the covers).*

(A short time later).

RAG DOLL # 23: Laura, Laura . . . *(Again and more insistently).* Laura, Laura . . . *(Only light is on the rag doll, as LAURA rubs her eyes in disbelief).*

LAURA: *(Sleepily).* Please go away . . . Oh . . . Oh! You're another one. *(To herself).* I guess Mrs. Smith and I overdid it with the anchovies on that pizza . . . Okay, say your piece and then please go . . .

RAG DOLL # 23: You may not understand my tale, Laura. I was given by the McKenzies, quite a while ago on Christmas Eve, to a little girl in a poor, poor family. You probably can't imagine how poor "poor" is. They lived in a tarpaper shack down by Rusty Creek. Her father worked part-time and was sick from emphysema which he got down in the copper mines. She was six and had never had a doll of her own. Their Christmas feast was some fish from the creek and cornbread with coffee. That year was the first she could go to Sunday School at the little church and tell the other girls what she got for Christmas. She's in high school now. She's working at a restaurant to support her family, and wants to be a nurse. When she loses confidence she holds me yet . . . and somehow she keeps on . . . I'd like to think I help by listening . . . But you with all your riches, you probably don't understand . . . Be thankful: this night be thankful to God . . . Oh, oh dear! My time is up. I'm going . . . *(Voice weaker).* going . . . be thankful this Yuletide . . . *(Lights out as **RAG DOLL** disappears).*

LAURA: What am I, Scrooge or something? What do I need with this "Christmas Carol" business? I could have any of three different versions — including *(Sits and stares thoughtfully into space).* Charles Laughton — right here on my videotape player. I don't need this. But I'd give up a car and a horse to have mother and father home on Christmas — to be a family again; to open our presents together; sing some carols; and to trim our own tree, stuff our own turkey . . . *(Sleepily).* I'd like that . . . *(Goes back to sleep).*

(After a short time another doll appears, lighted by a single source of light).

RAG DOLL #1: Laura, Laura! *(**LAURA** covers her head and moans).* Laura, Laura!

LAURA: *(She sits up, looking both bewildered and disgusted).* I suppose you've got a story to tell too. *(Sighs).* Fire away . . . and then, please, please go away . . .

RAG DOLL #1: I am the first of the dolls. Mr. and Mrs. McKenzie were to give me to their daughter on her third Christmas. Mrs. McKenzie added a lot of love as she sewed me for their only daughter. She knew they could have no more children. I was in a package under the tree when the little girl was taken ill. The doctors, and even a specialist over in High City, could not save her. Early in January she died, without ever regaining consciousness. I was thrown in a closet. They were in deep grief. There was no insurance. Mr. McKenzie sold the large market he had just built, in order to pay the bills. They bought an old store downtown. Finally, in December of the next year, they decided to give the doll to a little girl who had polio and could just barely hold me with her little hands — they were so twisted by the disease. They did more, too, as the girl's family struggled along with hospitals and doctors. So I was the first doll — a symbol of hope for a girl and her family. And I was a symbol of life after the dark grief and despair of that couple. They hit on the idea because as children both of them had wanted simple gifts they never got: Mrs. McKenzie, a flute to play at church; Mr. McKenzie, a wind-up train with cars and a circle of track. You don't know how much nerve it took for the old man to come here . . . but I hope you feel their love at this holy season. Be glad, Laura, be glad for this gift of love . . .

LAURA: I, I don't know what to say. I didn't know . . .

RAG DOLL #1: Of course you didn't know. But I must go now. I hope you find love and meaning in special, simple things, along with your riches . . . Good night; sleep well now *(Weaker)*. Good night . . . *(Lights out; doll leaves and **LAURA** falls back to sleep).*

NARRATOR: *(Lights now up a little)*. It is now early dawn on Christmas Day. The snow outside has stopped and every twig on every tree is covered. Down by the bay, on the beach below the house, a group of children sing as they walk from the church on the point back to their homes in the village.

CAROLERS: *(Sing "Joy to the World;" as they sing **LAURA** rises, tenderly picks up the doll and holds it, as she looks out the window and listens; they move further away and sing "Jingle Bells;" lights out as the singing stops, **LAURA** remains at the window)*.

NARRATOR: It is now the day after Christmas. Mr. & Mrs. McKenzie are again sitting by the stove in their store. Gerald is absent-mindedly sweeping with a broom. Outside, the day is sunny and the snow on the street is turning to slush. Icicles are forming on the eaves over the window. Snow is pushed back from the sidewalk in front of the store.

MR. McKENZIE: *(To* **MRS. Mc***).* Well, Martha, maybe we carried this doll-business too far. In a way I can't blame the poor girl. What right did I have to think she could appreciate such an unexpected and simple gift? Mebbie this doll — number 37 as I count — should be the last one. Mebbie we should just sell this place and move to Florida . . .

GERALD: Thirty-six out of thirty-seven ain't bad, Mr. McKenzie. I was mighty proud to go with you to deliver the present. Who knows, maybe next year . . .

MR. McKENZIE: Thanks, Gerald but I don't know . . .

MAID: *(Enters the store, carrying an envelope).* Good afternoon, Mr. and Mrs. McKenzie. I have a note for you.

MR. McKENZIE: *(Opens letter, adjusts glasses and reads aloud)*: Dear Mr. & Mrs. McKenzie, I want to thank you for your fine gift. Also, I apologize for my abruptness when you delivered the doll. I have remembered part of my life I had forgotten. When I was little, Dad got rich. One year I asked for a dolly to play with. I was happy when I got a dozen dolls and a huge, lighted doll house full of furniture. Because of my parents' love for me I have never wanted for anything, and I have enjoyed this.

Yet, your little gift has reminded me of love's simple gifts, and I thank you for your courage in presenting it to me.

You will make me happy if you both will see Mr. Short over at the department store. He has a flute and a model train laid back for you. Please take these gifts, even if you no longer want them. That would please me. I don't understand exactly how, but I know Mrs. McKenzie often thinks of playing the flute in church. And I have a feeling that you, Mr. McKenzie, look at the corner of your basement and think of building a railroad, but then say "But I'm too old . . . " Maybe at Christmas we're never too young or too old. Maybe at Christmas it is never too late.

Merry Christmas,
Laura Hibbing

(They are silent for a while).

GERALD: How 'bout that? Thirty-seven out of thirty-seven.

MRS. McKENZIE: I've got some material in mind for another doll.

MR. McKENZIE: I think that's safe. Because, you know what fine gift we've just been given?

MRS. McKENZIE: Yes, I think I know.

MR. McKENZIE: Faith. Faith in real and simple love. For a while there I thought love would run out, after thirty-six years. *(Dabs his eyes with a handkerchief).* Shame on me for such pride. Not in thirty-seven years, or thirty-seven times thirty-seven!

(Lights down).